AMERICAN PLACES
From Vision to Reality

Grand Central Terminal

by Kevin Blake

Consultant: Anthony W. Robins
Author of *Grand Central Terminal: 100 Years of a New York Landmark*

BEARPORT
PUBLISHING

New York, New York

Credits

Cover, © Pigprox/Dreamstime; 4–5, Public Domain; 5, NYPL Digital Collections/Public Domain; 6, © Library of Congress; 7, © Library of Congress; 8T, Public Domain; 8B, © Rebius/Shutterstock; 9, © Library of Congress; 10, Public Domain; 11, © Bailey-Cooper Photography/Alamy; 12, © Detroit Publishing Co./Library of Congress; 13T, © Rachel Bert/AGE Fotostock; 13B, © SM Photography/Alamy; 14, Public Domain; 15T, © IRA BLOCK/National Geographic Creative; 15B, © John Duricka/AP Images; 16L, © Felix Lipov/Alamy; 16R, © Library of Congress; 17, © Augustin Pasquet; 18L, © Delphotos/Alamy; 18RT, © Jorn Pilon/Shutterstock; 18RB, © KAZMAT/Shutterstock; 19, © Detroit Publishing Co./Library of Congress; 20–21, © redswept/Shutterstock; 22, © MTA Metro-North Railroad; 23T, © Everett Historical/Shutterstock; 23B, © Ritu Manoj Jethani/Shutterstock; 24, © Dave Pickoff/AP Images; 25L, © Richard Drew/AP Images; 25RT, © Richard Drew/AP Images; 25RB, © Anthony Behar/Sipa USA/AP Images; 26, © mizoula/iStock; 27, © Pongpon Rinthaisong; 28–29, © TTstudio/Shutterstock; 31, © Felix Lipov/Shutterstock.

Publisher: Kenn Goin
Senior Editor: Joyce Tavolacci
Creative Director: Spencer Brinker
Photo Researcher: Thomas Persano

Library of Congress Cataloging-in-Publication Data

Names: Blake, Kevin, 1978– author.
Title: Grand Central Terminal / by Kevin Blake.
Description: New York : Bearport Publishing Company, Inc., 2018. | Series: American places | Includes bibliographical references and index. |
Identifiers: LCCN 2017039239 (print) | LCCN 2017041948 (ebook) | ISBN 9781684024940 (ebook) | ISBN 9781684024360 (library)
Subjects: LCSH: Grand Central Terminal (New York, N.Y.)—Juvenile literature. | New York (N.Y.)—Buildings, structures, etc.—Juvenile literature. | Manhattan (New York, N.Y.)—Buildings, structures, etc.—Juvenile literature.
Classification: LCC TF302.N7 (ebook) | LCC TF302.N7 B59 2018 (print) | DDC 385.3/14097471—dc23
LC record available at https://lccn.loc.gov/2017039239

For more information, write to Bearport Publishing Company, Inc., 45 West 21st Street, Suite 3B, New York, New York 10010.
Printed in the United States of America.

10 9 8 7 6 5 4 3 2 1

Contents

All Aboard! 4

Deadly Accident 6

A Big Dig 8

Transportation Palace 10

People Traffic 12

Train Traffic 14

The Station's Secrets 16

Main Concourse 18

A Heavenly View 20

Disrepair 22

Save Our Station! 24

Gateway 26

Grand Central Terminal: By the Numbers . . . 28

Glossary 30

Bibliography 31

Read More 31

Learn More Online 31

Index 32

About the Author 32

All Aboard!

At the stroke of midnight on February 2, 1913, Grand Central **Terminal** opened in New York City. At the time, it was the largest and most **luxurious** train station in the world. During the day, more than 150,000 people pushed through its shiny doors. They gasped at the building's size, beauty, and **technological** wonders.

An illustration from an old postcard that shows Grand Central Terminal soon after it opened

The **enormous** terminal covered an area equal to 50 football fields. A maze of more than 30 miles (48 km) of railroad tracks snaked underneath the building. In addition, the trains and terminal were powered by electricity—making it one of the first all-electric stations. After seeing it, a reporter called it "not only the greatest station in the United States, but the greatest station, of any type, in the world!"

People streaming in and out of Grand Central Terminal

The first train to leave Grand Central Terminal was the Boston Express No. 2 at 12:01 AM. It's said that a person named F. M. Lahm bought the first ticket.

Deadly Accident

Grand Central Terminal (GCT) was not the first train station built on this site in New York City. In 1871, a station called Grand Central **Depot** stood where GCT currently stands. Over the years, as train traffic grew, the depot was rebuilt into a larger building called Grand Central Station.

Grand Central Depot stood from 1871 until 1899.

The trains that stopped at Grand Central Station ran on tracks that cut through the **bustling** city. Accidents were common. Sometimes, the trains hit people crossing the street. Also, the coal-powered trains spewed thick, black smoke into the air. This made it difficult for the train **engineers** to see other trains. On January 8, 1902, disaster struck. Two trains **collided**, killing 15 passengers. New York desperately needed a safer and cleaner system to move people in and out of the busy city.

A train accident involving a coal-powered steam engine

Grand Central Terminal is known as a terminal—rather than a station or depot—because all trains start or end at the building.

A Big Dig

An engineer named William J. Wilgus had a brilliant idea—put the railroad tracks underground and electrify the trains. The wealthy family that owned the New York Central Railroad—the Vanderbilts—loved the idea. Electric trains were faster and cleaner, which would be better for the city and its residents.

William J. Wilgus, the chief engineer of the New York Central Railroad

A steam engine spews thick, black smoke into the air.

Putting the tracks underground, however, wouldn't be easy. It meant **demolishing** buildings and digging 90 feet (27 m) into the ground to make room for the tracks. Despite the difficulties, the decision was made to go ahead with the plan. Each day, hundreds of tons of dirt were dug out of the middle of the city—or enough to fill up 300 railway cars!

Digging up the ground for the new train station

To build Grand Central Terminal, workers removed enough dirt to fill up the 102-story Empire State Building four times!

Transportation Palace

The railroad company also wanted a new main building that was beautiful and truly grand. **Architects** from around the country sent in plans for the new terminal. Some even proposed building a 60-story skyscraper! Finally, with input from the Vanderbilts, two teams of architects were selected to work together on the project. They were Reed & Stem and Warren & Wetmore.

The architects' drawing for Grand Central Terminal

The architects designed a huge, **classical** building with tall columns and giant curved windows. At the top of the station, they planned to install a 1,500-ton (1,361 mt) stone sculpture called *Transportation*. It would show three Roman gods, representing strength, speed, and trade. On the outside of the building, the architects decided to use creamy gray **limestone** from Indiana.

A huge stained glass clock was placed underneath the sculpture. It was made by Tiffany & Co.—a famous jewelry and glass company.

People Traffic

Grand Central Terminal would be more than just a beautiful building. It would be highly **functional**, too. The architects thought about the best way to move thousands of busy travelers quickly and efficiently through the station. What they came up with was a simple yet amazing **innovation**—ramps! By using **sloping** surfaces instead of stairs, passengers would be able to get around and reach the train tracks more easily.

This photo of Grand Central Terminal dates from 1912.

To build ramps at just the right slope, engineers studied how different types of people walked. They studied the steps of "lean men . . . fat men . . . women with babies . . . and all other types of travelers." Then the architects and engineers designed the perfect ramps for what would become the busiest railroad station in the world.

Ramps at Grand Central Terminal

The traffic ramp outside GCT

The architects even designed a ramp outside the station. It allows vehicles to travel easily around the massive building.

Train Traffic

Getting people in and around Grand Central Terminal wasn't the designers' only problem to solve. With 67 different tracks and hundreds of trains arriving and departing each day, keeping the trains moving safely and on time required careful planning. The engineers at GCT added a clever new feature—tracks that looped around in a circle. These circular tracks let trains turn around quickly to avoid traffic jams.

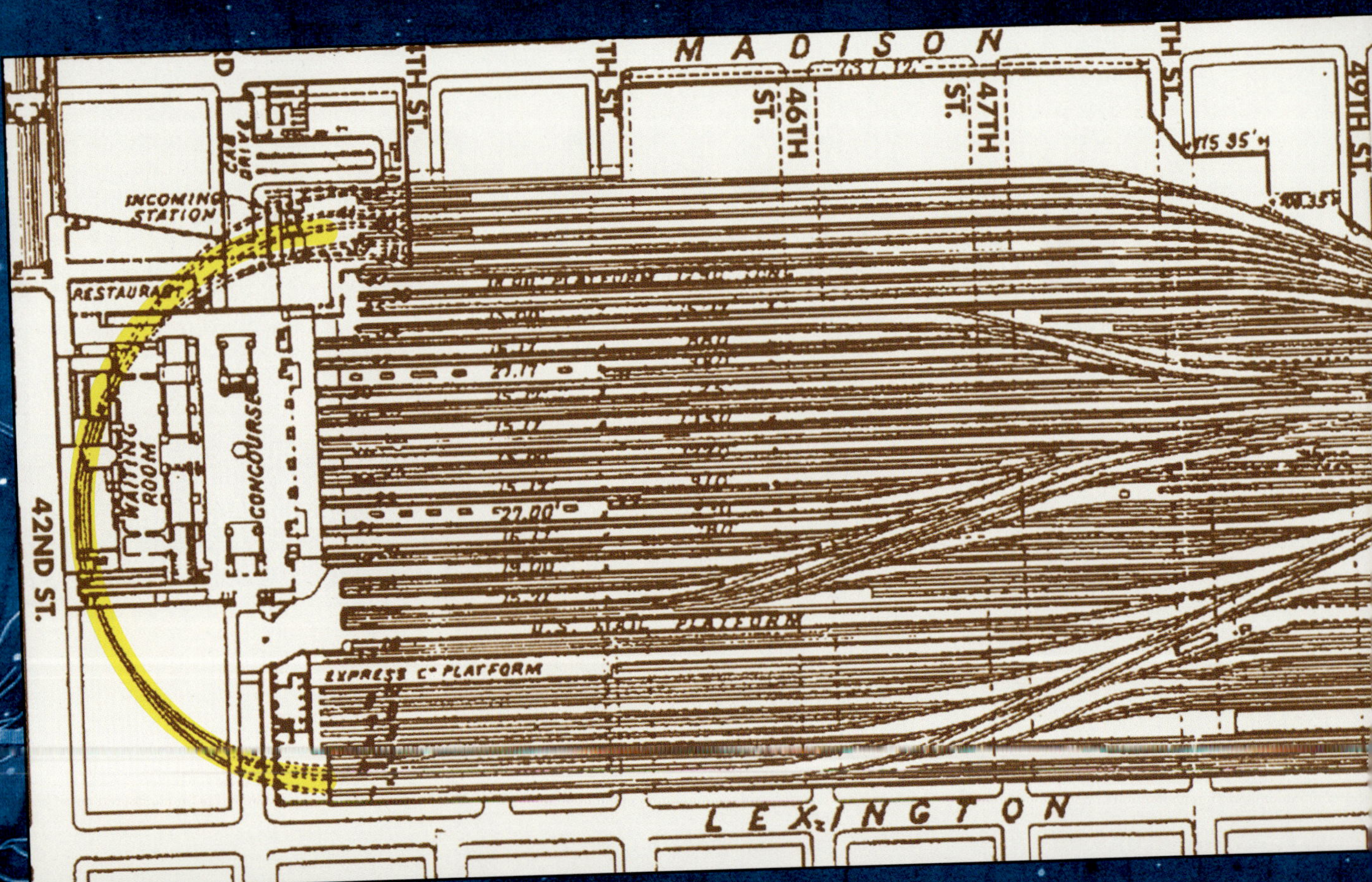

This old map shows the looping tracks at Grand Central Terminal.

To prevent accidents and keep trains on the right tracks, the engineers built the largest **traffic control** system ever made. They constructed five control towers to **monitor** traffic. The main tower had 400 levers that were used to direct where each train went. Teams of workers would monitor the trains and tracks around the clock to make sure that everything ran smoothly and on time.

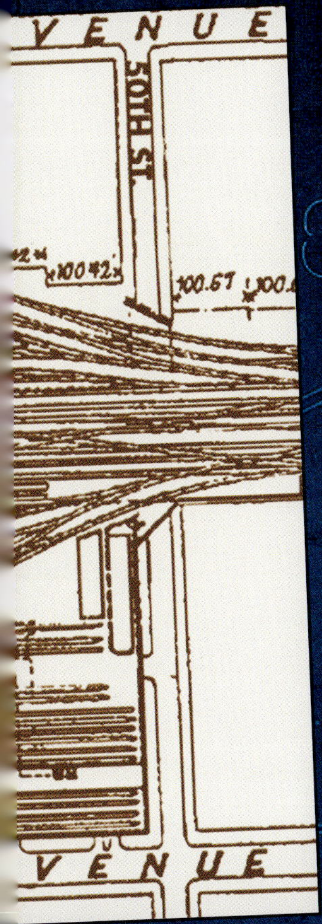

Operators inside the traffic control room at Grand Central Terminal

A passenger train pulling into GCT in 1967

Today, during the morning rush hour, a train arrives at Grand Central Terminal about every 58 seconds.

The Station's Secrets

Many years ago, workers directing traffic at Grand Central Terminal knew they had to keep one track—Track 61—clear. This track, which used to be a storage area, connected GCT to the Waldorf-Astoria Hotel a few blocks away. Only very special people were allowed to use the track, including a famous army general—and the president of the United States! In 1944, President Franklin D. Roosevelt rode on Track 61 after giving a speech at the hotel.

Track 61, which is no longer in use

President Franklin D. Roosevelt

Track 61 isn't the only mysterious part of Grand Central. Deep below the tracks is a basement level called M42. On this secret floor are four "off" buttons that years ago could have been used to shut down electricity to GCT and halt all train traffic in case of an emergency. It's said that only a handful of people ever knew about this master shutoff.

According to one story, during **World War II**, enemy German spies landed in New York. They were on a mission to enter M42 and shut down America's major railway terminal. They were quickly captured.

Inside the M42 area below Grand Central Terminal

Main Concourse

For everyday passengers arriving at Grand Central Terminal, the first stop was usually the **Main Concourse**. Many considered this huge space to be the grandest in the entire station. It included a soaring ceiling and ten sparkling **chandeliers**. Each one glowed with 132 light bulbs. In the center of the room stood an information booth topped with a large brass clock with four faces made of milk-colored glass.

The Main Concourse today, where many of the building's original features still exist

One of the chandeliers

The clock at the center of the Main Concourse

The top of the clock features an acorn—the family symbol of the Vanderbilts.

In addition to the beautiful **decor**, luxurious **amenities** awaited passengers in the Main Concourse. There were private dressing rooms with maid service as well as barbershops. In addition, people could dine at fancy restaurants. There was a waiting room that became known as the "kissing gallery" because loved ones would often greet one another there.

The Oyster Bar is a famous seafood restaurant that opened at GCT in 1913. It's still in business today.

A Heavenly View

The designers of Grand Central Terminal placed one of the most beautiful features of the Main Concourse above people's heads! French artist Paul-César Helleu designed the ceiling to look like the starry sky. Workers painted it a deep greenish-blue color. Then they added 2,500 glittering gold stars to form **constellations** and symbols called zodiac signs.

The ceiling above Grand Central's Main Concourse

There was only one problem—the sky was painted backward! The constellations Taurus and Gemini are reversed from where they actually are in the sky. There's been a long **debate** about why the artist would do this. Some people think the ceiling was painted that way on purpose. They believe the very powerful Vanderbilts wanted the sky to appear as if seen from the heavens, rather than from a human's point of view on the ground. Other people think it was just a mistake.

Tiny lights were also placed on GCT's ceiling so that some of the stars appear to glow like real stars!

Disrepair

Sadly, many decades after it opened, Grand Central Terminal fell into terrible **disrepair**. In the 1960s and 1970s, visitors could not even see the Main Concourse's beautiful ceiling because a layer of thick black grime covered it. In addition, homeless people began using the terminal as a shelter.

People sleeping on benches at GCT in the 1970s

The grime on the Main Concourse's ceiling wasn't due to the trains. Instead, the problem was caused by **pollution** from decades of cigarette smoke.

Some people thought it was time to tear down Grand Central Terminal and replace it with a modern building. The other major train station across town—Pennsylvania Station—had been demolished in 1963 and a tall glass building put up in its place. Architects drew up plans for a skyscraper to replace Grand Central. However, many people remembered how beautiful the terminal once was—and they were willing to fight to save it.

The old Penn Station

The new Penn Station

Save Our Station!

New Yorkers did not want to see such a stunning and historic building torn down. A group led by former First Lady Jacqueline Kennedy Onassis fought to save Grand Central Terminal. She and others argued that the terminal was not only beautiful but an essential part of New York's history. Architect Philip Johnson famously said, "Europe has its **cathedrals**, and we have Grand Central Station." In 1978, the battle ended. Instead of being demolished, Grand Central would be **restored**!

Jacqueline Kennedy Onassis (center) and other supporters, including architect Philip Johnson (right), stand in front of Grand Central Terminal in 1975.

Over the next several years, more than 400 million dollars was spent to restore the terminal to its former **splendor**. The ceiling was scrubbed and repainted. Crumbling stones were replaced with new ones. Special light bulbs were installed in the ceiling stars to make them shine more brightly.

During restoration, safety netting was placed on the ceiling and walls to catch falling debris.

Cleaning the dirty ceiling

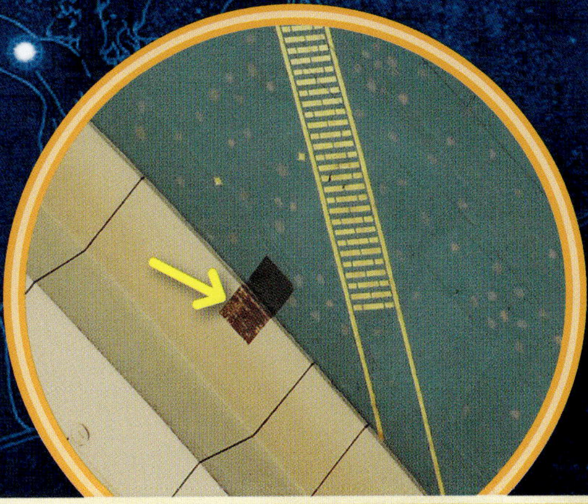

As a reminder of how filthy it once was, workers left a small dirty patch on the ceiling.

Gateway

Today, Grand Central Terminal welcomes hundreds of thousands of train passengers each weekday. If you add in the people who come to the station to eat, shop, and work, that number jumps to 750,000! It's as if the entire population of Alaska enters the building each day.

Passengers hurry to their trains at America's biggest train station.

More than 50 million people visit Grand Central Terminal each year!

However, Grand Central Terminal is more than just a busy train station. It's an architectural wonder that inspires people who enter its doors and gaze up at its starry ceiling. It's also an engineering marvel that moves people in and out of New York City. More than 100 years later, it remains one of the world's greatest train stations.

Grand Central Terminal is located on 42nd Street in Manhattan.

Grand Central Terminal

BY THE NUMBERS

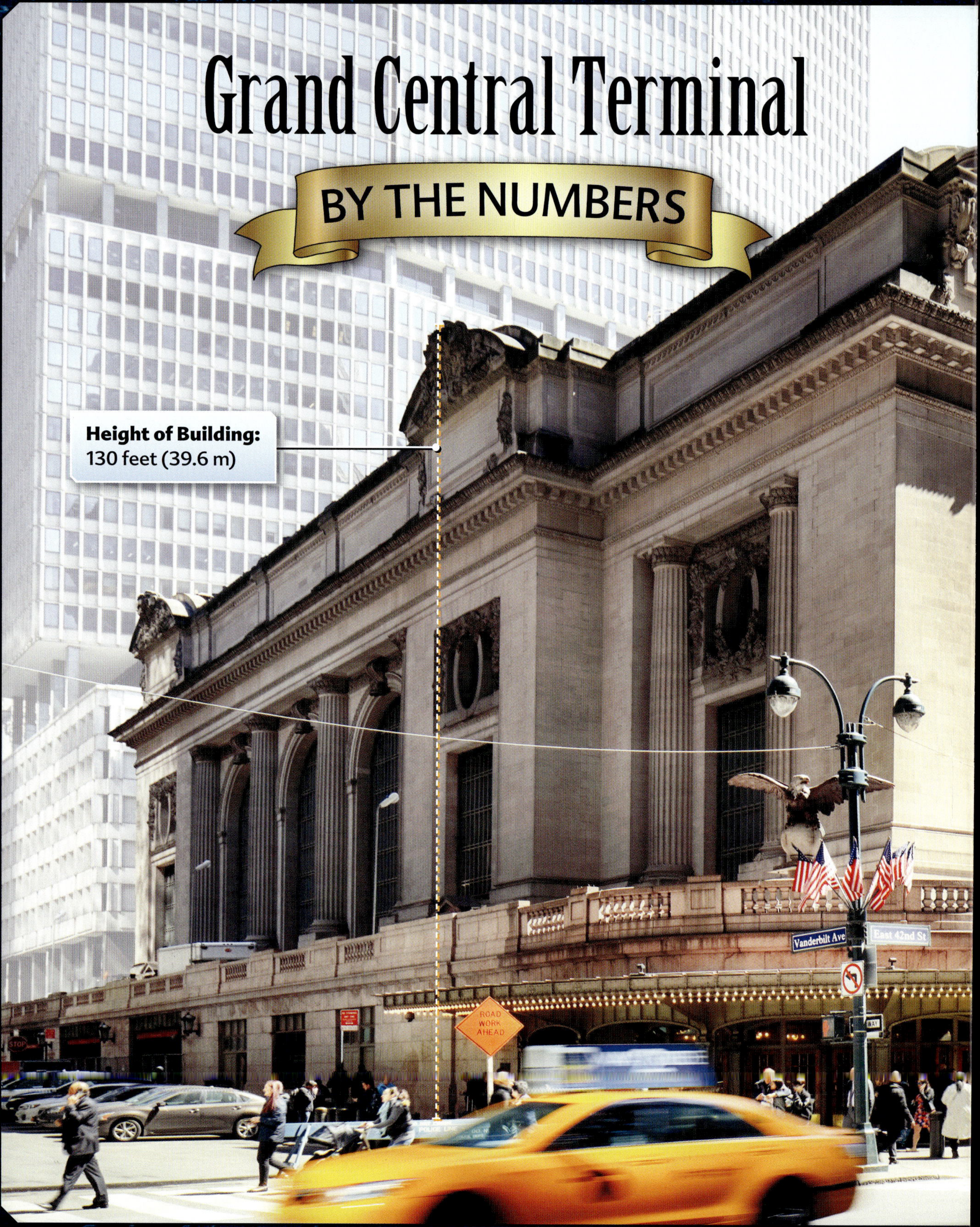

Height of Building:
130 feet (39.6 m)

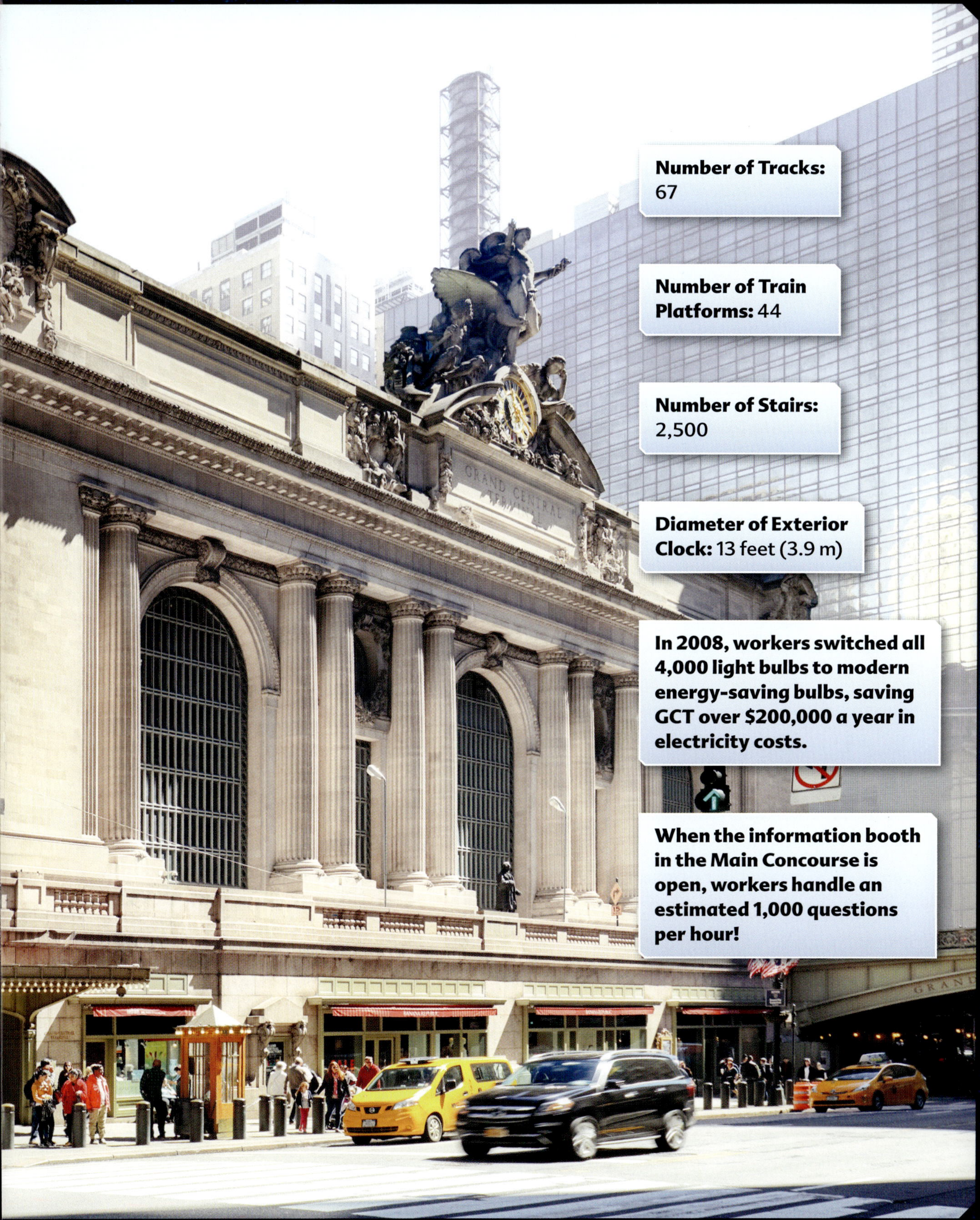

Number of Tracks: 67

Number of Train Platforms: 44

Number of Stairs: 2,500

Diameter of Exterior Clock: 13 feet (3.9 m)

In 2008, workers switched all 4,000 light bulbs to modern energy-saving bulbs, saving GCT over $200,000 a year in electricity costs.

When the information booth in the Main Concourse is open, workers handle an estimated 1,000 questions per hour!

Glossary

amenities (uh-MEN-i-teez) things that provide comfort, convenience, or pleasure

architects (AR-ki-tekts) people who design buildings

bustling (BUHSS-ling) filled with activity and movement

cathedrals (kuh-THEE-druhls) large, important churches

chandeliers (shan-de-LEERZ) light fixtures that are hung from the ceiling

classical (KLAS-i-kuhl) in the traditional style of ancient Greece or Rome

collided (kuh-LIDE-id) crashed into something

constellations (kon-stuh-LEY-shuns) groups of stars

debate (dih-BEYT) a discussion or argument between two sides

decor (dey-KAWR) decoration

demolishing (dih-MOL-ush-ing) tearing down something

depot (DEE-poh) a railroad station

disrepair (dis-ri-PAIR) in bad condition; needs fixing

engineers (en-juh-NEERZ) people trained to design or operate machines such as trains and vehicles

enormous (ih-NAWR-muhs) huge

functional (FUHNGK-shuh-nuhl) designed to work well

innovation (in-uh-VEY-shun) a new idea or invention

limestone (LIME-stohn) a stone often used for buildings

luxurious (luhg-ZHOO-ree-us) fancy and expensive

main concourse (MAIN KON-kawrss) a large open space in the center of a building

monitor (MON-i-ter) to watch and listen

pollution (puh-LOO-shuhn) harmful chemicals and other materials that damage the air, water, or soil

restored (ree-STAWRD) brought something back to its former condition

sloping (SLOHP-ing) at an angle or slant

splendor (SPLEN-dur) great beauty

technological (tek-nuh-LOJ-i-kuhl) related to science and engineering

terminal (TUR-muh-nuhl) a station at either end of a transportation line

traffic control (TRAF-ik kun-TROHL) a process by which trains or other moving objects are directed

World War II (WURLD WOR TOO) a worldwide conflict that lasted from 1939 to 1945

Bibliography

Roberts, Sam. "100 Years of Grandeur—The Birth of Grand Central Terminal." *The New York Times* (January 18, 2013).

Robins, Anthony W. *Grand Central Terminal: 100 Years of a New York Landmark.* New York: Abrams (2013).

Wallace, Mike. *Greater Gotham: A History of New York City from 1898 to 1919.* New York: Oxford (2017).

Read More

Blake, Kevin. *Statue of Liberty (American Places).* New York: Bearport (2016).

Goldish, Meish. *One World Trade Center (American Places).* New York: Bearport (2018).

Stanley, Ed. *Grand Central Terminal–Gateway to New York City.* New York: Mondo (2003).

Learn More Online

To learn more about Grand Central Terminal, visit:
www.bearportpublishing.com/AmericanPlaces

Index

ceiling 18, 20–21, 22, 25, 27
chandeliers 18
clock (Information Booth) 18

Gemini (constellation) 21
Grand Central Depot (1871–1899) 6
Grand Central Oyster Bar and Restaurant 19
Grand Central Station (1899–1913) 6–7

Helleu, Paul-César 20–21

Johnson, Philip 24

lights 18, 21, 29
limestone 11

M42 level 17
Main Concourse 18–19, 20, 22, 29

New York City 4, 6–7, 24, 27

Onassis, Jacqueline Kennedy 24

Pennsylvania Station 23
platforms 29
pollution 7, 8, 22

ramps 12–13
Reed & Stem 10
Roosevelt, Franklin D. 16

Taurus (constellation) 21
Track 61 16–17
traffic control 15
Transportation statue 11

Vanderbilt family 8, 10, 18, 21

Warren & Wetmore 10
Wilgus, William J. 8
World War II 17

About the Author

Kevin Blake has written many nonfiction books for kids. He lives in Providence, Rhode Island, with his wife, Melissa, son, Sam, and daughter, Ilana.